To

From

Other books in this series:

HAPPY ANNIVERSARY
To someone special, celebrating your
   LOVELY NEW BABY
To a very special BROTHER
To a very special DAD
To a very special DAUGHTER
To a very special FRIEND
To a very special GRANDMA
To a very special GRANDPA
Wishing you HAPPINESS

To my very special HUSBAND
Someone very special...
   TO THE ONE I LOVE
To a very special MOTHER
To a very special SISTER
To a very special SON
To a very special TEACHER
Wishing you happiness
   FOR YOUR WEDDING
To my very special WIFE

Published in 1996 by Helen Exley Giftbooks in Great Britain.
This revised edition published in 2008

12 11 10 9 8 7 6 5 4 3

ISBN 13: 978-1-84634-295-0

Helen Exley Giftbooks, 16 Chalk Hill, Watford, Herts WD19 4BG, UK.
www.helenexleygiftbooks.com

To a very special®
GRANDSON

ILLUSTRATIONS BY JULIETTE CLARKE.
WRITTEN BY PAM BROWN.
EDITED BY HELEN EXLEY.

It is very easy to get out of the way
of laughing as the years pass.
One settles for a smile – until
a grandson comes along –
and one learns to laugh again.

HELEN EXLEY®

A NEW LIFE

You have turned our settled lives upside down.
You have flung open windows
closed against the cold.
You have let in blazing sunlight on
our gently shaded lives.
You have brought a shout of joy
into our ordered quietness.
You have given us back life and hope
and adventure.

You were the best of bonuses.
I never thought to be a grandparent
– but here you are.
And I am very nearly young again.

My grandson was four months old.
Scarcely arrived.
And yet his eyes explored
my face and knew me and he gave me a smile
of joy so absolute it was worth
a lifetime's waiting.

Cold winds turn the last of the leaves
and a thin rain patters down.
It could have been a sad time, a time of loss.
But then you came –
a promise of summers still to come.

How nice to be hugged
by a huge grandson – it makes
an overweight old lady feel slender again.

HAPPY DAYS

The door crashes open
and a small boy hurtles in with a torrent
of extraordinary news.
And how can gloom survive?

The sounds to lift a
grandparent's heart are the pounding of
small feet up the path and the
hammering of small fists on the door.
How dull life was before you came.
How much joy
is packed into a little boy.

One arrives – and there is a face at
the window – a small face
that lights up in absolute astonishment
and delight. It is the greatest joy.
It is the greatest gift.
Thank you for that.

There are many kinds of happiness.
Many kinds of love.
But nothing to surpass the delight of a
little child running into
one's arms – their face alight with joy.

You are the gold at the end of our rainbow.

WHIRLWINDS AND CHAOS

Grandsons are always on the move.
They ricochet from walls and trees and
furniture. They swirl like dust-devils. They leap
and plunge like fish. They are a blur.
They are noise made visible.
And sometimes, suddenly, and for the blinking
of an eye, they come to rest beside a grandma.
And engulf her in a hug.

Grandsons take you on roller-coasters and
bumper cars. Grandsons help you up and over
rocks. Grandsons assure you that scuba diving is
a doddle. Grandsons encourage you up castle
keeps, windmills and skyscrapers.
Grandsons give you a turn on their mountain
bikes. Grandsons take you to rock concerts.
Grandsons give you a spin
in their first sports car. Grandsons sit
with you on walls when you go a funny green.

It is very hard sometimes to love a grandson
with the in-built destructive abilities of
an elephant, the love of dust inherent in
a buffalo, the appetite of a grizzly fattening
itself for winter. But you do. You do.

Going for a walk with a grandson is like
being an ancient sailing ship
being towed by an over enthusiastic tugboat.

How can a day be dull
when one has a grandson?

TOGETHER!

The phone rings, "Grandma? Guess what…?"
And then what amazements follow….

No one can lose contact with the
contemporary world when they have a
grandson who comes visiting.
Grandsons are always greatly surprised to
discover that ancient grandparents know
quite a lot of useful stuff.

It's extraordinary what new interests
grandparents acquire in old age.
Rap and Soul and Salsa.
Bungee jumping. Snowboarding.
And, in turn, their grandsons gain
new insights into the way
old gramophones used to play.
A liking for early Fords.
And a taste for newly-baked bread.

The greatest pleasure grandparents can have
is for a grandson to say:
"This book looks interesting –
can I borrow it?"
or "Could you spare this for a little while?"
or "Can I have a turn at this?"
or "May I take a cutting from this rose?"
To share with you is joy.
Our lives link in the
giving, in the taking. In the smiles.

IT'S LOVE!

Never forget, not for a single moment,
how much we love you.
Wear our love lightly. Never let it be a burden.
Let it be an extra coverlet in the cold,
dark days – and a pleasant
breeze about you when life is good.

We are such little creatures, you and I, yet we
hold in us mystery. For we are capable of love.
In the flicker of time that we exist, we will love
each other – and that love, my dear, can never
be lost. It reaches to the ends of all that is.

Grandsons are far too busy to come
to the door to see a grandma or grandad leave
– for they are Superman or Robin Hood or a
creature from the Black Lagoon.
But just before the car pulls out,
or you set off along the road, there is a
hammering of feet – and a shining face.
And a breathless "Luf you."
Which is the best of gifts to bear away.

There are no kisses as wet, as sticky
and as heartfelt
as the kisses of a little grandchild.

THE YEARS ARE NOT LOST

You walk with me a little way,
matching your pace to mine –
then on an impulse race away,
leaping and turning like a hare,
finding scents upon the breeze
that I have lost long since.
You are a part of summer, part of
the dazzle and dapple, the shifting
leaves, the sway of grasses,
the flicker of birds
across the cloud-flecked sky.

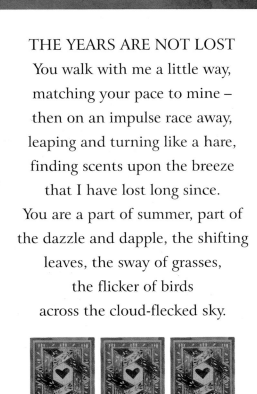

And through you I remember
how it was in the lost years –
and share your laughter.
You circle back and take my hand.
And talk as if you'd never left me.
And I know, because of you,
that however dark the world seems,
however full of grief and loss,
to live is the greatest privilege.
To breathe the air, to walk in the
sun – to hold a grandchild's hand.

TWO FRIENDS

You are my friend. You always have been
– ever since you took my finger when
you were brand new.
Ever since you learned to smile.
We've shared a lot.
First teeth. Scuffed knees. Birthdays.
We've wondered at the paws of newborn kittens.
Mumps. I remember mumps.
I remember the time that we all got lost.
And the time we ran and ran for the bus
and I puffed and puffed and you
made them wait for me.
Dear Grandson. I had begun to be old –
but you told me not to.
So I'm trying very hard.
How neatly your hand fits into mine.
Wait till I get my keys –
and we will go out and find a new adventure.

Grandparents and grandsons have
a specially snug place all of their own,
where there are cuddles
and secrets and buttered scones.

Dear Lad. If you ever need someone
with time to listen...
if you ever need a bolt-hole –
here's one waiting.

AGE? WHAT IS AGE?!

Getting old comes as a surprise –
for inside, grandparents are still as young
as they ever were.
So many people do not understand this
simple fact – but you are not bamboozled.
You look into our eyes and
recognize us as the same age as yourself.

A lot of people stop loving you
when you get old and lined and peppered
with little brown blotches.
But grandsons like you that way.

It's strange to think you love
as a grandparent someone I scarcely recognize
in the mirror. For you, a grandparent
has white-spattered hair, a double chin,
a comfortable shape; while I know myself to be
thirty, slim, dark-haired and agile.
Still – by the way you take me off to have
adventures, I suspect that somehow
you know about the person who's forced
to wear this daft disguise.

Grandsons like to get on your knee
and examine your face, inch by wrinkled inch.
The veins, the wrinkles, the sneaky little
whiskers fascinate them. It's disconcerting. But
who cares? They love you exactly as you are.

JUST THE EXCUSE I NEED

Grandsons are the best excuse yet for playing
with mud and water.

Thank you for being my excuse to do
all the things I love to do.
With you, I can roll down sand-dunes,
fly kites, wade into ponds,
skim stones, climb trees,
do the polka, eat lollipops and licorice
bootlaces, and read Winnie the Pooh and
Treasure Island once again.
Thank heavens for grandsons.
They give grandads a reason to play snap.
They give grandmas a reason to bake cakes.

A grandson like you is the perfect alibi
to do all the things old fuddy-duddies
think undignified.
Who needs dignity!

Grandsons allow you to stand and watch
mechanical diggers, even in the rain.
Grandsons give you the chance to yell at
football games and eat sticky buns in teashops
and talk to bus drivers and try out
computer games. Grandsons make it all right
to toast muffins over bonfires in the garden.
Grandsons take one camping.
Grandsons share their toffees.

ALWAYS HERE FOR YOU

Grandmas and grandads exist to
listen and to keep secrets.
And to offer advice you can take or
ignore just as you wish.
With never a string attached.

If you're miserable or furious –
come round to see me.
We can be miserable and furious together.
Or talk it out.
Or just eat my currant cake.

Dear Lad. Never let disappointments
or resentments or sadness gnaw away
at your heart, believing
no one else can understand.
Grandads and grandmas may seem infinitely
old – but the memories of their childhood
are as vivid to them as if those times
were only yesterday. They have stood
exactly where you stand.
If you need us, we are always here.

Here's a heart to love you,
a mind to understand you, ears to listen and
arms to hug. All at your disposal. Always.

MY WISHES FOR YOU

I wish you happiness
with all my heart.
Laughter, smiles, love,
hope, contentment.
Joy in the ridiculous
and the sublime.
In little things and great.
But most of all
the happiness that comes
from mastery of a skill.
Which can outlast
even love itself.

I wish you so much, but most of all I wish you courage. Not battle-bravery, but the quiet courage that endures, survives and never loses hope. The courage that will sustain you through every darkness, the courage that will give strength to others. The courage that will turn what seems defeat into victory.

I have such hopes for you
– not fame or riches, though they may come, but the enthusiasm to make bold choices, to learn and experiment and make and do. To weather storms. To learn from failure. To discover goodness in other people.

I wish I could give you the lovely things lost in modern tumult – the silences, the scents of summer days, the velvet dark, the myriads of stars, the drift of butterflies, the quiet streets.

WITH ALL MY THANKS...
Thank you for scooping me into your life
– and making me a part of your
adventure.

One's children grow up and become
sensible and sophisticated – and,
however loving, a little weary with
one's stories – and a little sarcastic about
one's singing voice. But you ask for
my stories and delight in my songs!
Bless you!

Thank you for all those squidgy
kisses you gave me once – and the pecks
when you were growing. And the snuggly
ones you gave when I was sad.

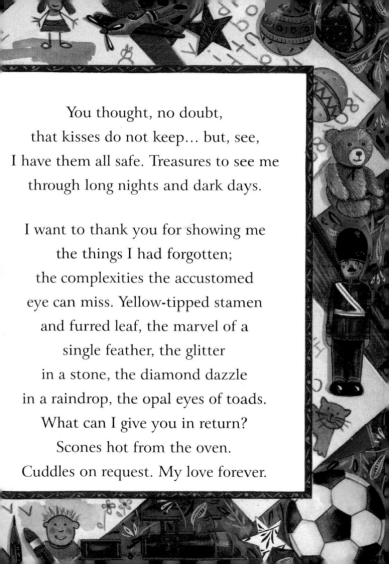

You thought, no doubt,
that kisses do not keep… but, see,
I have them all safe. Treasures to see me
through long nights and dark days.

I want to thank you for showing me
the things I had forgotten;
the complexities the accustomed
eye can miss. Yellow-tipped stamen
and furred leaf, the marvel of a
single feather, the glitter
in a stone, the diamond dazzle
in a raindrop, the opal eyes of toads.
What can I give you in return?
Scones hot from the oven.
Cuddles on request. My love forever.